A *Doonesbury* Book by

G.B. Trudeau

It's Supposed To Be Yellow, Pinhead

Selected Cartoons from
Ask for May, Settle for June Vol. 1

FAWCETT CREST • NEW YORK

A Fawcett Crest Book
Published by Ballantine Books
Copyright © 1981, 1982 by G. B. Trudeau

Library of Congress Catalog Card Number: 81-84328

ISBN 0-449-20193-7

This book comprises a portion of ASK FOR MAY, SETTLE FOR
JUNE, and is reprinted by arrangement with Holt, Rinehart and
Winston.

The cartoons in this book have appeared in newspapers in the United
States and abroad under the auspices of Universal Press Syndicate.

Manufactured in the United States of America

First Ballantine Books Edition: May 1983

10 9 8 7 6 5 4 3 2 1

It's Supposed To Be Yellow, Pinhead

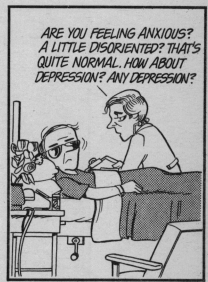

AHMAD AND ASIF? GOOD MEN, BOTH OF THEM. IF THEY HADN'T BEEN KEEPING AN EYE ON ME, THE CIA WOULD HAVE WASTED ME **MONTHS** AGO!

THAT REMINDS ME, I PROMISED I'D CALL THE GUYS AND LET THEM KNOW I'M OKAY..

TEXT-BOOK CASE.

I CONCUR.

GBTrudeau

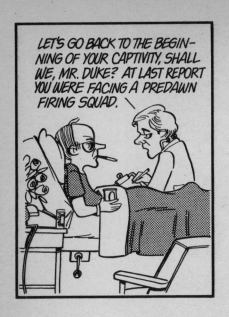

LET'S GO BACK TO THE BEGIN-
NING OF YOUR CAPTIVITY, SHALL
WE, MR. DUKE? AT LAST REPORT
YOU WERE FACING A PREDAWN
FIRING SQUAD.

RIGHT. AT THAT POINT, NEGOTIATIONS
HAD KIND OF BOGGED DOWN. I
WAS FORCED TO MAKE A LAST-DITCH
OFFER OF $250,000, WHICH IT TURNED
OUT WAS THE GOING RATE FOR A STAY
OF EXECUTION.

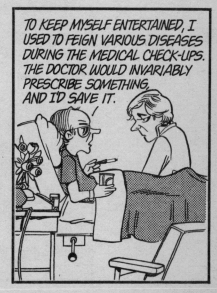

DOCTOR, WHAT SORT OF CONDITION IS THE 53RD HOSTAGE IN?

PHYSICALLY, HE SEEMS TO BE FINE..

PSYCHOLOGICALLY, THERE APPEAR TO BE SOME PROBLEMS. WHAT IS NOT CLEAR, HOWEVER, IS HOW MANY OF THEM EXISTED PRIOR TO HIS CAPTIVITY.

WELL, I GUESS EVERYONE'S HERE. WHO'S OUR FIRST WITNESS TODAY, DEAR?

A MR. SLACK-MEYER. HE JUST JOINED THE COUNCIL OF ECONOMIC ADVISERS.

REP. DAVENPORT

REP. GE

SLACKMEYER? HMM.. DON'T THINK I KNOW THAT NAME.

HE'S AN EXPERT IN TAX SHELTERS AND MONEY FUNDS.

REP. DAVENPORT

REP. G

WHETHER THE U.S. MEANT TO WIN THE VIETNAM WAR OR NOT, TODAY THERE IS GROWING PRESSURE TO FIND A WAR WE CAN WIN. U.S. STRATEGIST ABE LEVIN EXPLAINS HOW EL SALVADOR WAS SELECTED.

EL SALVADOR

IT WASN'T EASY. WE'D BEEN LOOKING FOR A PLACE TO DRAW THE LINE FOR WEEKS, BUT THERE JUST WEREN'T ANY CIVIL WARS ON THE FRONT PAGE. FINALLY, SOME GUY IN RESEARCH HIT ON EL SALVADOR.